SALLY LEIPER

MEMENTO

Poems and stories from a country life

SALLY LEIPER

MEMENTO

Poems and stories from a country life

MEREO
Cirencester

Mereo Books

1A The Wool Market Dyer Street Cirencester Gloucestershire GL7 2PR
An imprint of Memoirs Publishing www.mereobooks.com

MEMENTO: 978-1-86151-505-6

First published in Great Britain in 2015
by Mereo Books, an imprint of Memoirs Publishing

The address for Memoirs Publishing Group Limited can be found at
www.memoirspublishing.com

The Memoirs Publishing Group Ltd Reg. No. 7834348

The Memoirs Publishing Group supports both The Forest Stewardship Council® (FSC®) and the
PEFC® leading international forest-certification organisations. Our books carrying both the FSC
label and the PEFC® and are printed on FSC®-certified paper. FSC® is the only
forest-certification scheme supported by the leading environmental organisations including
Greenpeace. Our paper procurement policy can be found at
www.memoirspublishing.com/environment

Typeset in 10/17pt Bembo
by Wiltshire Associates Publisher Services Ltd. Printed and bound in Great Britain by
Printondemand-Worldwide, Peterborough PE2 6XD

CONTENTS

ABOUT THE AUTHOR

Sally Leiper was born Sally Ross in Aberdeen in 1935 and attended Albyn School there before going on to St Leonard's School in St Andrews. Back in Aberdeen, at Robert Gordon's College, she followed her father into a career in pharmacy, but wrote dog-related articles for the *Scottish Field* and various other publications over the 60s and 70s. During this time she bred and showed dogs from her Farmacy Kennel.

A short break from pharmacy became a much longer break when she and her husband, with twenty-one dogs, seven cats and a selection of poultry, moved to a small farm near Banchory. There they spent ten years – and that, as they say, is another story. In 1975 Sally became the Scottish correspondent for *Dog World*, a job which included the provision of a weekly column over thirty happy years. As she neared retirement, pharmacy became a part-time job and she was able to join the Westhill 50 Plus Creative Writing Group. Much of the work in this book stems from those cheerful and instructive fortnightly meetings.

ACKNOWLEDGEMENTS

This little collection of verse and prose covers a good many years of writing. During those years I have appreciated the help and encouragement given by family and friends. But most of all, I thank the members of the Westhill 50 Plus Creative Writers' Group and our ever-helpful tutors. To be required to produce a piece of verse or prose every two weeks during term time is a great stimulus to effort. I knew that I should have to read the result and then, after general discussion, hand it in to John Easton or Helen Posgate. Both these accomplished writers had the gift of truly constructive criticism, so that we could look forward to receiving their considered opinions.

The Fred Dragon stories were first told to my young niece, who made no criticism, but simply said, 'Tell me about Fred Dragon,' when I offered a bedtime story. So I wrote them down, and Fred has reappeared for two generations of family since then.

To my husband, John I can never really give enough of a Thank You. For more than fifty years he has faithfully read the drafts of not only verse and articles but the weekly column which I wrote for *Dog World* magazine for about thirty years. Long before the arrival of my first computer, he was my advisor, my spell-checker and my grammar checker too.

Sally Leiper

POEMS

CONFUSION

I am lost; in a dream.
Don't know which way to go.
Things are not what they seem.
White the earth – dark the snow.

It's a negative view,
And I don't recommend it.
With a letter to post,
I can't think how to send it.

I should turn and go home,
But I've lost my direction.
Perhaps I'll stay here,
Lost in deep introspection.

Has it happened at last?
Is my speech weird and garbled?
Have I ceased to talk sense?
Am I really dis-marbled?

Not just lost; I am trapped.
This is truly a blow.
I have been here before,
But where's here?
I don't know.

A SMALL 'LOST CHORD'

When I'm trapped in my own darkness and the walls are closing in,
When the fight that I have fought so hard seems hardly worth the win.
Then I need Your help to fight it and I ask You what to do.
'Come to Me,' I hear You answer, and I bring it all to You.
For I am floored, Lord.

All the pains and woes and worries,
All the heartaches and the fears.
All the knowledge of my failings,
All the dried and unshed tears.
All these things I bring to You, Lord, when there's nowhere else to go.
And I lay them down before You, and I feel the comfort grow.
I can feel the tension lessen and the peace come slowly through.
Like a small 'Lost Chord,' Lord.

NOSTALGIA

We bought some land near Banchory
And when we first were seen
They called us 'In-aboot-ers'
Though we came from Aberdeen.

They thought we would have ponies
And, perhaps, a goat or two,
But we had dogs and cats and hens,
For these were things we knew.

Quite soon we bought a flock of sheep
At the 'Little Michael Fair'.
But this produced a problem
How to get them home from there?

Our flock was only nine ewes big
And while we thought it over
A friendly farmer neighbour said
'Put them in my Land Rover.'

Those Blackface ewes were wild and free
Though they had looked such charmers.
But now we had some proper stock,
They called us 'hobby farmers'.

As time went by I bought a pup
And though but three months old,
Tib knew far more of the ways of sheep
Than I had e'er been told.

The summer passed and winter came
And, for my Silver Wedding,
I got a most unusual gift –
Three heifers in the steading.

As I look back upon those years
I know my views are tinted
I see them through a rosy glow
I think of joys unstinted.

I never think about the times
We lambed in driving snow.
I seldom now remember how
The old stock had to go.

Now Tib and I walk through the park
For there's no work to do.
But I keep those golden memories
Of a dream that once came true.

BIRDS

The WAGTAIL is a cheerful fellow
He comes in grey and pied and yellow.
He's never still, he's always bobbin'
I much prefer him to the robin.

Of HERONS I'm extremely fond
Although they raid my goldfish pond.
I like their solemn, careful ways
And plumage of assorted greys.

The MAGPIE's just a well-dressed crow.
His morals are extremely low.
He makes an unattractive sound
And small birds hide when he's around.

The CUCKOO is a horrid bird,
The sound it makes is quite absurd.
It hatches in another's nest
And then it murders all the rest.

The WREN is such a tiny bird,
You'd wonder that she could be heard.
But yet, with voice both loud and strong
She scolds you as you pass along.

The DIPPER has a style surprising.
You see him from the water rising.
He dives beneath the waterfall
And never minds the cold at all.

The JAY is in his Sunday best
On Monday, Tuesday and the rest.
His shout alarms the woodland folks.
His buried acorns grow to oaks.

AWAY

I walked beside the bluebell wood,
But the bluebells were broken and grey.
They were crushed beneath a rusting fridge
That someone had thrown AWAY.

I walked across the meadow
But no cow grazed the hay
For the cow had died of a plastic bag
That a tourist had thrown AWAY.

I walked beside the river
Where the otter used to play,
But the otter was dead of a hook and a line
That a fisherman threw AWAY.

It's sad that in our local park
The children no longer play
Because of the litter and broken glass
So carelessly thrown AWAY.

AWAY is the very easiest place
To throw your rubbish in.
You can see it wherever you happen to look
SO, LOOK FOR A RUBBISH BIN.

MILK PUDDING

Farola, semolina and the rest,
Milk puddings put my manners to the test.
At many a childhood, lunch those curds and whey
Would slither on the plate – soft, white and grey.
The sight, the touch, the smell of that dread plateful,
The very sound of it was hateful.

To leave some brought the risk of sudden skelpings,
To finish brought the risk of second helpings.

I have a fairly catholic taste in food,
But, to this day, I cannot eat milk pud.

WISDOM

My granny had a proverb for the start of every day
I still recall the wisdom of the things she used to say.
'Do as you would be done by, as you start to lift life's lid.
Do as you would be done by - or be done by as you did.'

'If you have nothing good to say, then nothing say at all.
The spoken word that's once been heard you never can recall.
And though you speak politely, you still can have your say.
Remember that an answer soft can turn the wrath away.'

My granny's favourite proverbs are many ages old.
To other generations, this wisdom has been told.
Now children press computer keys and wisdom they can see
But I still prefer the proverbs that my granny taught to me.

CHRISTMAS CHILD

Bigger things, newer things, more than last year,
That's the wish of Christmas for the Free World boy.
Green-eyed, square-eyed, thinking of the great fear
'Perhaps the shop is out of stock of the new computer toy.'

Smaller things, older things, even less than last year
That's the threat of Christmas for the Third World boy.
Wide-eyed, terrified, thinking of the great fear
Of bombs and guns and bullets that the men of war enjoy.

The Western child with game and screen lets last year's present rust.
The Eastern child, unclothed, unseen, picks rice grains from the dust.
For one of these the game of war can be switched off at will,
But the hungry, naked, frightened child sees killers really kill.

Edited and re-titled Game of War, November 2010.

WARTIME MEMORY

In the year of the war my Papa bought a car,
T'was a Talbot, the joy of his heart.
He would use all endeavour to keep it for ever,
He vowed that they never would part.

It was shiny and sleek, with a front like a beak
And twin chrome-plated horns like two talons.
It could laugh at the weather; it had seats of brown leather
And a tank that held twenty-one gallons.
When war was declared, most car owners despaired

And they walked – for the sake of the nation.
But, safe from the barrage, cocooned in the garage,
The car slept and Dad walked to the station.

But on one day each year there was wonder and cheer,
When Dad brought out his one can of fuel.
With a teaspoonful in and a sly, rueful grin,
He proceeded to break his own rule.

Then the great engine purred, what a joy to be heard,
To the gate – then poor Dad's heart would harden.
For that trip of the year was no journey, I fear.
But was simply a trip round the garden.
But at last peace came round and some petrol was found
We piled into the car double quick.
Father drove out the gate; it was smooth, it was great,
But when he drove fast – I was sick!

TOPSY

Now she sleeps
There in the garden where she loved to be.
Deep she sleeps.
And, in the spring-time when the garden wakes,

We'll plant a tree
Where, still, she sleeps.
There, in the garden where she played with me.

A special dog, though all may special be,
Topps with her beauty and her love of life
Was dear to me.

No harm did she.
All her life long she and the world were friends.
Not quite ten years of life,
How suddenly it ends.

Death, when so gently given, was her release.
Though there is pain for us, her pain has ceased.
Our grief is sharp for Topps, but it will fade.
Our memories will keep her – happy in that garden
Where throughout her life she played.

In memory of 'Topsy the Turvy', a Belgian Shepherd Tervueren, 1982-1990
Edited several times; now called NUNC DIMITTIS.

NUNC DIMITTIS

Now let me sleep
Quiet, in the woodland where I loved to be.
There let me rest;
Free from the pain, the fear, the sympathy.

I shall sleep quietly there,
For I have lived my life.
A happy time, blessed in so many ways.
Now, as I sleep, remember happy days.

Plant there a tree.
And when it comes to leaf
Share in its joy – my joy.
Let peace replace your grief.

This is a variation of the Topsy poem written for myself.

DENIAL

Gethsemane.

'I know you not.'

The denial of Christ.

Made in fear of the forces of power.

Guantanamo.

'I believe you not.'

The denial of liberty.

Made in fear by the forces of power.

DEAR GHOSTS

I close my eyes, and they are here.

Come from that secret place where old friends sleep.

They stir at my call.

We are together now.

Topsy and Tib; Scottie and Merry;

So many faithful friends.

Now we can go wherever memory takes us.

Up to the hill?

Down through the woodland's shady places?

They are here with me.

But dreams must end.

My dear ghosts melt and fade

Back to that kindly place where they will wait for me again.

Waiting, I know - until I come to them.

THE GOOD, THE BAD
AND THE TASTY

They say that all the things we eat

Are much too salty or too sweet

And rules by which we must abide

Are thrown at us from every side.

Now even all our politicians

Declaim to us like dietitians.

They have a quite simplistic view,

'If food tastes good – it's bad for you.'

Eat no more sweets and crisps, for you

Will one day rue it if you do.

To save your heart from risk of flutter,

Abandon even bread and butter.

Those bacon rolls and eggs and ham,

Those suet puds with loads of jam,
Those joys may boost your central heating,
But they're not recommended eating.
Soon, heavy footsteps in the hall,
Will mean the Food Man's come to call.
He'll represent the Nanny State
And want to check your dinner plate.

So give yourself a Christmas treat.
Have something really GOOD to eat.
But, oh beware; for as you do,
You'll know how BAD it is for you.

TECHNOCHONDRIA

When I awoke, I felt so poorly
I thought I must be ill – and, surely
I could find out, from the 'net'
If this would be my worst ill yet.

I could not give my aches a name
But Google to the rescue came.
I typed my symptoms by recall,
And found they fitted ailments all.
I surfed each 'itis' and each 'osis'.

I found the facts, and the supposes.
I found an 'ology' beside
And listed what those queer names hide.

By night time I was in a tizzy.
Worrying kept my mind so busy
I hardly slept, and then not well
Having a nightmare straight from Hell.

The next day dawned; the sun did shine.
I woke up, feeling simply fine.
Who needs Google's mad suggestion?
I guess I'd just had indigestion.

THE CURSE OF THE CRUMBLING CUSP

When you're old, it's a fact – but it's true
Your incisors and molars are too.
What you used to do gladly,
You now think of sadly,
When a trip to the dentist is due.

He will look and consider and say,
'Are you fully insured – or just pay?'

'If you think you can brave it, I will try to save it
But I'm sure it will crumble away.'

Then he made an explorat'ry poke.
I yelled, and he solemnly spoke:
'If you're happy to pay, I'll remove it today.
So he did,
And I'm happy,
But broke.

A LITTLE HILL

It surely was an afterthought
When the Deeside hills were made
But I could lift my eyes to it,
Whenever I needed aid.
It's just a very little hill
A hillock, a hump, or less,
But to sit and to look at the view from there
Was a certain cure for stress.
I could sit and absorb the silence
In that truly blessed place
For even a little hill will do,
When you seek God's peace and grace.

December 2005

WORK

Of all the jobs that I have tried,
The shepherd's is the best.
Its satisfaction rating
It is way above the rest.
The work is hard, the hours are long
And when the weather's bad,
The little lambs are cold and wet
And they and I are sad.
But suddenly the sun comes out.
The dark clouds roll away.
And suddenly the lambs are fine,
They gambol, jump and play.
Now, every shepherd needs a dog,
A collie dog, so clever.
From birth they know the ways of sheep
And they forget them never.
A pharmacist I was for years
A journalist as well
But my few short years of shepherding
Gave me many tales to tell.

BE PREPARED

I take a lot of tablets
For all my aches and pains
I need some for my allergies
And for my fear of planes,
So when I plan my holidays
I see the doctor first
I like to have a chat with him
For I always fear the worst.
I've had my vaccinations
For pneumonia and flu
And there's one in case of typhoid,
And for hepatitis too.
I go to all the chemists' shops
And hunt along the shelves.
I speak to lots of pharmacists
About what they use themselves.
At last it is departure time
For my annual getaway.
I've packed my biggest medicine bag,
And I'm off to Cruden Bay!

EASTER

Sorrow and grieving
Born of believing.
Sharing the loss
And the pain of the Cross.

The grave's inspection
The Resurrection.
Freed from our sinning.
A New Beginning.

CATS IN SPRING

(OR 'Here we go gathering birds in May'.)

Felines awake! Your time is here,
For the songbirds nest in the spring of the year
There are nestlings for me and fledglings for you
And we'll get them before the magpies do.

THE HAIKU

I am going mad.
I roam the house, muttering.
I have Haikuism.

Haikuism is a disease of the creative system.

It is spread by suggestion and is extremely addictive.

Symptoms include distraction from the normal patterns of life and,

in severe cases, the sufferer may be seen to be counting upon their

fingers while muttering 'five – seven – five' in an agitated manner.

Haikuism is an ancient disease which originated in the East.

Poets and authors are particularly susceptible.

It has no known cure, but may be self-limiting when the brain

becomes surfeited and, in desperation, shuts down its versifying circuits.

GOOD AND BAD

Us and them

Cowboys and Indians

Cops and robbers

Our soldiers and their soldiers

Good and bad.

All so simple.

For I was a child.

Us and them?

White people and coloured people

Victims and aggressors

Patriots and terrorists.

Good and bad?

No longer simple.

For I have grown old.

MILLIE'S POEM

Now she sleeps.

There, in the woodland, where she loved to be.

A peaceful sleep; and when the woodland wakes

We'll plant a tree.

In that quiet woodland, where she walked with me.

No harm did she.

All her life long she and the world were friends.

A life of joy and love; now, peacefully it ends.

Though grief is sharp for Millie, it will fade.

Our memories will keep her happy in that woodland

Where throughout her life, she played.

Millie Whippet, 24th October 2000 to 5th September 2014.

NUMBER PLEASE!

For Mistress Isobel Dalrymple
The telephone had once been simple
She knew her callers one and all,
The phone exchange was in her hall.
Before the days of World War 2
She was the postal mistress too
Her cottage, next the village shop,
Saw friends and strangers pass or stop.
She seldom needed a correction
When asked to make a phone connection
To doctor, rector, nurse or squire,
Or 999 for police or fire.
She longed for that familiar dial,
That once she twirled with a smile
The keys now pressed for every call,
Seemed far too close – and far too small.
She pressed ten keys with concentration,
Though more in hope than expectation
That someone human might be there;
To answer her with thought and care.
There was a voice – not loud or clear
Which said, 'I'm sorry, I'm not here,
Speak clearly when you hear the tone,
I'll call you when I get back home.'

Alas, for ageing Miss Dalrymple

Nothing in life is quite as simple

As when she once asked, 'Number please,'

And they were only fours and threes.

MOVING DAY

(With apologies to 'Old Macdonald.')

John and Sally had some fun on that moving day

Although they only had to go twenty miles away.

With a 'put this here' and a 'put that there', dogs and people everywhere.

John and Sally had some fun on that moving day.

Oh John and Sally had some fun on that moving day

With labradors and setters too and whippets all a-play

With a 'mew mew' there and a 'cluck cluck' there,

Cats and chickens everywhere

John and Sally had some fun on that moving day.

Oh John and Sally had some fun on that moving day

When, with twenty one dogs, seven cats and a whole lot of poultry

They finally moved away.

And off they went to the farm.

THE WISHING POOL

I sit beside the Wishing Pool,
The sun is warm, the water cool,
The only sound, the leaves a-swish
What shall I wish?
The Wishing Pool's a magic place.
Above it, waters freely race
But it is secret, still and deep,
It seems to sleep.
I have seen otters playing here,
And trout lie by the banks so sheer.
A bright kingfisher once I saw,
But then – no more.
Just once, upon a winter's day
I saw an ermine stoat at play.
White upon white, with leap and turn
It crossed the burn.
Still as the seasons come and go,
The pool reflects the sun's bright glow
Now springtime primrose, pale and shy
Smiles at the sky.
I sit beside the pool and dream.
My dogs are playing in the stream.
Although I sit there on my own,
I'm not alone.

MONA LISA

She touched the box in her pocket - and smiled
A Mona Lisa smile.
Her thoughts were her own; she would not share
She would take no part in the trial.
He stood in the dock, bemused and scared
Could his innocence still be proved?
He had loved her once and he loved her still
But he knew she would not be moved.

One last little piece of evidence
Was needed to set him free
But he dared not glance at his one-time love
Up there in the gallery.
She touched the box in her pocket - and smiled.
She stood up – and walked away.
'Guilty as charged,' ruled the magistrate.
There was nothing the lad could say.

THE GAME OF WAR

Bright eyed, square-eyed, a boy plays his computer game
A game where all is fantasy, and the good defeat the bad
Wide-eyed, terrified, as bombs explode and bullets maim,
Another boy seeks safety in a world gone truly mad.
The Western child, with careless greed, lets last year's playthings rust
The Eastern child, with desperate hands, picks rice grains from the dust.
For one of these, the game of war can be switched off at will.
But the hungry, naked, frightened child sees killers really kill.

WHEEZLES AND SNEEZLES

When Christopher Robin had wheezles and sneezles
They bundled him into his bed
But in this day and age we allow colds to rage,
And we sneeze in the office instead.
But at last when our sneezles have turned into wheezles
To the doctor we stagger and say
Oh I have done my best, but it's into my chest
And I'm coughing all night and all day
I've tried lemon and honey, but my nose is still runny,

Give me antibiotics I pray.

Despite Day and Night Nurse, I've got steadily worse

I would even be willing to pay.

I did think I could cope, but I'm now losing hope

Oh, I think I am fading away

There's a party tonight and I must feel all right

So please will you cure me today?

STORIES

THE ATTIC

'Oh dear,' moaned the Attic Controller, 'Whatever next?' He looked across the attic to the door, at which a queue was forming. 'Come in, come in. I can't think where I'm going to put you all.'

The queue shuffled forward and there was a bit of shoving and pushing as three of larger members came to the front.

'All right now, take your time,' protested the Controller. 'How many new Capitals this morning?'

'Three of us,' snapped the Capital letters together, 'G, B and T.'

'T?' squeaked the Controller. 'Do you mean T as in Thank you?'

'That's right,' admitted the T. 'And here are G and B from Great and Britain.'

'Oh dear, oh dear,' sighed the Controller. 'Doesn't anyone write letters by hand any more?'

'TEXT,' hissed a voice, and the whole attic seemed to quiver at the sound of that dread word. The Capital Letters shrank visibly, and it needed only a small sign from the Controller to send them slinking across the dusty floor to where a collection of their fellows were stacked against the wall beside a chest full of redundant apostrophes.

'And who let you in here?' demanded the Attic Controller. He glowered at a very small, new arrival who was sidling towards a stack of shallow drawers. 'You can't be obsolete.'

The Hyphen sniffed dismally and nodded his broad, flattened head. 'Yes,' he sobbed. 'Obsolete, that's me! It's in the new OED.' His words brought a gasp from the whole queue, for the OED was their bible.

'Side-saddle,' whispered the poor Hyphen. 'Leap-frog. Six thousand words to be listed without a single one of us in their middles.' His voice rose to a piercing squeal. 'And WHY?' There was a hushed and expectant pause as capital letters, punctuation marks and small words waited breathlessly for his explanation.

'Laziness!' Proclaimed the Hyphen in despairing tones. 'People simply can't be bothered to reach across to press my key.' He reached the drawers, scrambled to the edge of the shallowest one, slithered in sideways and slammed it shut behind him.

'Phew!' breathed the Controller. 'I hope that's all for this morning.'

At that moment his attention was drawn to a strange sound, like a hiccup. He looked about him and saw nothing, but then the sound changed to a sob and, as he peered over his desk he saw crouched in front of it a word so small that it had been invisible from where he sat.

The Controller came round to the front of the desk and bent down to give the little word an encouraging pat. 'Are you lost?' he asked. 'You surely are too ordinary to be in my attic. Who are you, anyway?

'I'm a TOO,' sniffed the little word. 'I feel so insulted. Really, I think I've been killed off.'

'Tell us about it.' The Controller's voice trembled. What was going to happen to the English language if a word like TOO was to become obsolete? TWOs came often to his attic nowadays as they fell victim to the overpowering force of the NUMBERS who replaced them – but TOO?

The little word's voice was barely audible. 'There is a new sticker in a car's back window.' he whispered. 'It is quite official; it even has a police badge. It says "RU2 CLOSE?"'

'Oh dear!' moaned the Attic Controller. 'Whatever next!'

THE MAT

The cat sat on the mat.

He was an old cat and his black fur, once glossy with health and careful attention, was now dull and somewhat tufted. His golden eyes were half closed and his body sagged, then jerked back to wakefulness. He was tired, very tired, but he fought against the urge to sleep, for then he must curl himself upon the hated mat; that hygienic, newly-washed square of chenille which carried the ultimate indignity of the words BATH MAT woven into its stain-free, germ-free, cat-resistant fabric.

Why could he not have his own old bed? Why should that familiar, padded place of comfort be denied him? It was not very clean, for it held the long-established essence of his own personality, but it was, most of all, a place of privacy and safety in a strangely hostile situation.

It was not unusual for the cat's owner to leave him alone in the house. There was a cat flap from the kitchen and Dick's next door neighbour came daily to see to his food and to tidy the litter tray that he used only if he could not face a rain-lashed garden.

But this time was different. This time he had not been left alone, for Dick's mother had offered to stay in the house during his absence.

The cat knew well that the woman did not like him. She had been to the house before and he had heard her voice, shrill with disapproval as she berated her son for his careless housekeeping and his slovenly ways. She protested that he cared only for his car and his cat. He had owned both for eleven years and it was true that the cat was respected and cared for while the treasured car – a Morgan 4/4 registered in 1994 – gleamed with loving attention.

The cat's golden gaze slid towards the chair which was his second choice of resting place. The woman was in the kitchen and he heard the hiss of the spray as it propelled the choking mist of floral disinfectant that rendered the room unbearable to him.

Silently he moved closer to the chair; he tensed himself, then, with a huge effort, he sprang clear over the padded arm to land, not on a welcoming cushion, but on a pile of books purposely placed to ensure that they and he would topple to the floor.

The resulting noise brought the woman from the kitchen and her strident, scolding voice was the final straw. Shocked beyond his fear, he turned with back arched and ears flattened, a hissing, spitting fury that sent her running to her own sanctuary and the kitchen door slammed between them. With no escape to his cat flap, he fled into the hall and through the only other open door.

He had never been encouraged to go into Dick's bedroom but in his blind panic he scrabbled up on to the bed to collapse against another furry body which, strangely, gave no evidence of resenting his arrival.

Gradually his breathing quietened and his heaving sides settled to an occasional quiver. The occupant of the bed was a large soft toy, treasured in childhood and retained only from sentiment. It was a spaniel dog, equipped with a zip fastener along its back which could be opened to give access to a padded pouch for the tidy storing of a child's pyjamas.

The spaniel had a somewhat moth-eaten appearance and his one remaining eye gazed glassily at the cat, who - comfortable at last - curled himself against this new-found friend and slept.

The woman came to the bedroom doorway still scolding, but she heard the deep low growl of the cat and with a helpless gesture she flung the pink bath mat on to the bed, for she was genuinely horrified at the sight of that horrid creature actually lying there.

Dick returned to find his flat in a state of unaccustomed order. Everything that could be polished, gleamed. Everything that could be vacuumed had been vacuumed until it had had its very heart sucked from it. Books were no longer piled upon their shelves but stood to attention, arranged, regardless of subject matter, strictly in order of size.

In the little kitchen chrome surfaces shone coldly brilliant and the floor showed a pattern he had forgotten was there. Of the cat's bed there was no sign.

His question was swiftly answered.

"That cat!" she snapped. "That cat's a devil, a dirty, smelly, ferocious devil, and that old bed was so filthy I put it where it belonged, in the dustbin with all the other rubbish."

Dick's voice rose to a squeak of panic "What do you mean by rubbish?"

"Just rubbish," she repeated. "Old shoes, old cushions, old magazines. This place has been a disgrace for years and I never got a real chance to tidy it till I had this time here on my own. Except," she added venomously, "for that cat."

Dick stared at his mother, the colour draining from his face. His voice cracked. "Have you tidied everywhere?"

"No I have not. That cat won't let me into your bedroom."

He was through the hall as she spoke and as he flung open the door the cat reared up on the bed, only to stare at him for a moment before scrambling over the toy dog to greet him.

Dick stood for a moment taking in the familiar details of the one room that had escaped his mother's onslaught.

Her voice came from the kitchen, shrill and demanding. "Put that cat outside - and bring that moth-eaten old dog down with you. I would have had it in the dustbin if I could have got past that spitting fury."

But Dick was not listening. He had grabbed the old toy dog and with trembling hands he pulled the zipper to extract a crumpled T-shirt from the pouch. Wrapped within the T-shirt was a wad of notes. They amounted to nineteen thousand three hundred and ninety pounds; the price received for the sale of the Morgan, which had taken place late on the evening before he left for the States.

He turned to the cat, now purring luxuriously beside him. "Thanks old friend and guardian," he whispered. "This will buy you the best bed ever."

He caught sight of the pink chenille square lying where his mother had thrown it across the foot of the bed.

"And," he added, "we'll get rid of that damned mat."

TIME BOMB

The sunlit bay, with its mile of golden sand, might have been designed to fulfil the dreams of any child, but Ryan thought it was boring. He dawdled along the tideline, hands thrust deep in the pockets of his jeans, and gazed resentfully at the far end of the bay where the sand gave way to cliffs and the dunes became rocks

Glorious rocks! Jagged and sharp or wave-washed and smooth, they held the promise of secret pools where weird creatures scuttled and swam, awaiting the return of the tide or the depredations of small boys.

But the boys who lazed on the rocks were big boys. You had to be at least ten to be a member of the Rockers gang. Ryan was almost eleven, but he was a scrawny boy and the Rockers, with the careless cruelty of childhood, had spurned his advances.

"Too small! Too small!" they had chanted. "Go and join the Beach Boys. They're just your size."

So Ryan was forced to join the little boys' gang, where he

soon contrived to become their leader. But still he yearned to be a Rocker. To do wicked things; to thrust fishing hooks into the crushed bodies of crabs; to pull sea anemones from their havens and to hurl fist-sized, sea-rounded stones at the resident gulls as they swooped and squabbled, noisy as the boys themselves.

There were just four members of the Beach Boys gang, but today they too had decided that they could be wicked – if only by pretence. So Ryan had sent his troops to gather such props as would convince the world that the gang was a force to be reckoned with. They would be a marine, an outlaw, a commando, and their leader would be a Secret Agent.

Having made these decisions the boys had dispersed to scrounge such evidence of their new identities as came to hand. Ryan had gone home, where lunch – cold pizza and a bag of crisps - awaited him. But he had been quite unable to find anything that a Secret Agent might use while upon his desperate adventures.

James Bond had an Aston Martin and a beautiful girlfriend, but neither of these essentials was available to Ryan. Then he remembered something and he changed his mind – he knew now what he would be, and it would be really wicked.

He went up to his bedroom and dived under the bed where his treasure box lay hidden. In the box was an oblong of heavy material wrapped in plastic film. He had found it on the high tide mark a couple of weeks before and had been intrigued by its weight. He had intended to ask his father what the stuff might be, but when he got home his parents were watching the television and he did not like to interrupt.

The news item referred to various toxic materials which had been washed up on a beach some miles north of his home area. Ryan was not sure what toxic meant, but in his imagination he became a heroic member of a bomb disposal team and the package became a wondrously dangerous trophy.

The Beach Boys met at their den, an old concrete pill-box, a relic of the war. It was partially filled with sand but they had cleared a space into which they could wriggle. They had lit a fire of driftwood there but the low roof had caused the smoke to billow down instead of up and they had emerged in a hurry coughing and choking.

The Marine showed off his beret (sadly, black rather than green) and of course, a gun. The Outlaw had a bow and arrow, the Commando a balaclava and a plastic sheath -knife. These were displayed, and then they waited for Ryan, who announced, "I'm not a Secret Agent – I'm a Terrorist!"

His subordinates were impressed, but seemed less so when all the terrorist could show to back up his claim was a lump of something heavy, wrapped in plastic and tied with a sort of cord to his dad's best leather belt.

"What is it anyway?" They peered at Ryan in the gloom.

"Gunpowder – or something like it," declared the terrorist. "I found it on the beach. It makes you a Time Bomber; you put it on you and you get on a bus or a plane and you light the fuse."

Here, to the admiration of the gang, he produced his father's lighter and applied the little flame to the end of the cord.

The roar of the explosion brought the distant Rockers to their feet.

The gulls rose, screaming, to wheel together above the old pill box wherein lay the burned and broken bodies of four small boys.

February 2004

This ending upset the members of the Writers' Group so much that I did a 'happy' one. But I think this is better.

A LITTLE GREEN MAN

'Little green men indeed!' snorted Ada. She arranged her twelve-foot body along the bench and glared at her companion. 'You watch far too much Earth telly.'

Edna sighed. 'I suppose you are right. But have you seen their science programmes, with all that ancient technology?'

'Their technology may be ancient,' snapped Ada, 'but their passion for sending probes into space is becoming a perfect bother. A queer wee machine with wheels landed in my yard not so long ago and I had to get Bert to exterminate it. That Bert!' She gave another snort. 'He wanted to keep it to play with, but I said, 'Put it away, boy. You don't know where it's been.'

A loud thump was heard and the room shook. 'Oh no!' she cried. 'Not another landing.'

Bert wriggled in. He clutched a doll-like figure whose sickly face could be seen through the spherical helmet. 'Look what I found,' he cried. 'Can I keep this one?'

Edna stared at Ada. 'It's a little green man!'

I WILL SEE YOU TOMORROW

The music was very faint now, but Elsie was no longer able – or indeed willing – to distinguish between what was real and what was memory. Her sight too had faded but, in her mind's eye, she saw the great column of the Cenotaph, and before it the tiny, black-clad figure of the queen.

The solemn strains of *Nimrod* swelled and dipped at the command of the Royal Marines' music master, but Elsie was lost in her memories of long ago.

The pictures moved jerkily, like the silent films which she and Harry had watched together, in the back row of the cinema. Then Harry had gone to war, and Elsie had taken her nursing skills to serve the unending streams of wounded soldiers, sailors and airmen; so many of whom were being remembered now at the Cenotaph and at monuments all over Britain. They had almost come through unscathed, but in January of '45 Harry had been brought home, battered and almost blinded, and dependent on those skills which Elsie could provide. Harry was a fighter; he had bitterly hated this need for help and had lashed out verbally at his wife and at his son, Hugh.

It was Illis, the gentle guide dog, who had given independence back to Harry, slowly

and patiently gaining his trust. Elsie smiled mistily at the memory of the two of them setting out fearlessly to the shop or the pub. They had had ten years together, but Illis' retirement marked the beginning of the end of Harry's battle. Too frail to take on a new dog, he refused even to attend the local Remembrance Day parade where they had marched together.

So Elsie and Harry had turned to the national ceremony on television; but he was not with her as she prayed for the safety of Hugh's daughter Annie who, like her grandfather, had gone off to war.

How thankful Elsie had been as she had watched the return of the TA service men and women and how proud, as Annie marched to Birkhall to be welcomed home by the Prince of Wales.

Big Ben sounded the first stroke of eleven and London fell silent. Elsie slipped a little deeper into her nest of pillows. Annie, sitting at the bedside, took one frail hand in a warm clasp.

As his damaged sight had faded, Harry had said each night, 'see you tomorrow, girl.'

Lately, Elsie had remembered this more often, and last night Harry had smiled at her, though his words were a little different.

'I will see you tomorrow,' he had said, and held out his hand.

Annie felt the faintest pressure. Then, as the signal gun boomed and the Last Post sounded, Elsie took Harry's hand and went with him.

YELLOW DOG DINGO

His back against the bole of an ancient oak and his face turned to the east, he sat in silence, waiting for the sunrise and hoping for real warmth, more real than the passing heat brought by the dregs left in the bottle.

Slowly he opened stiff fingers and gazed at the small yellow tablets that filled his palm. 'Benzos' – Diazepam tablets, filched from a carrier bag of prescription drugs left carelessly open on a bus seat beside the owner. 'Pity they were only yellow and not blue,' he thought, knowing well the strengths indicated by the colours.

The eastern sky lightened slowly from grey to primrose. He lifted the bottle, tipped it to his lips, then threw it down with unnecessary violence. Cider was OK, but not to be compared with vodka. 'Yellow again,' he grumbled. That blasted colour had haunted him.

He remembered what some well-read clown of a policeman had called him years ago when his yellow hair had been distinctive – not fashionable as it was now: 'Yellow Dog Dingo. ' But when he had found a cellmate who knew the origin of the name, he discovered that it was not so rude after all. 'Yellow Dog Dingo,' said the story. 'Very much run after and very hard to catch.'

But they had caught him. Then and again, so often that the life inside and out merged in his memory to a single bad dream of drugs leading to depression, leading to crime, leading back to court.

But this crime had been different. Cold, wet, hungry and racked with the need for drug relief, he had gone into the church thinking only of shelter. He had not expected the woman to rise up from her knees just as he put his hand on the steel candlestick. She had let out a yell that triggered an instinctive reaction and he had swung the heavy object with such force that he swept the altar cloth to the floor. When he looked down at her inert body, panic took him, and he pulled the cloth over her bloodied face.

He fled from the church, from the street, from the town, but he could not flee from the memory.

The sky had brightened from primrose to lemon and he felt a comforting touch of warmth on his face. He stretched out his arm to lift the cider bottle and discovered that the dregs would be sufficient for what was needed. He looked again at the yellow tablets, then threw the lot into his mouth and washed them down.

'Yellow Dog Dingo', he muttered. 'Not very hard to catch now.'

Soon the combination of drugs and alcohol began to take effect. His eyes closed and his body relaxed.

He was in a boat on a river. His hand moved to take the tiller, but he was too tired to bother. He let the current take him and now he floated without need of the boat.

Peaceful at last, he floated down the yellow river – down, down to the ultimate comfort of oblivion.

FRED DRAGON
AND THE PEPPERPOT

Long, long ago, in a land called Far Away, there lived a lonely dragon whose name was Fred. He was a handsome young dragon with green wings and red legs, and his body was all covered with silver scales.

Fred Dragon could fly very well and when he had practised for a while, he could make a fine, deep roar. But he had one terrible problem – he could not breathe flames from his mouth.

Again and again his father had told him what he must do.

"You must think very angry thoughts, Fred," he had said. "This will make you feel very hot and then, when you breathe a great roar, you will make a fine flame."

But Fred Dragon simply could not make himself feel angry. He liked everybody he knew and he could not think angry thoughts about dragons he liked.

When he grew up and he still could not breathe fire, Fred was teased by the other dragons and he got so sad that he went off to live by himself in a rather damp cave near the top of a rather high hill. He often thought how nice it would be to be warm and cheerful instead of cold and lonely.

When he was very sad he would heave a great sigh. When this happened a cloud of damp fog would come from his mouth, so the walls of his cave were quite drippy and sometimes the top of his hill was covered with fog and could not be seen from the village below.

One sunny morning in spring, Fred was lying outside his cave and thinking how nice it would be to have some company when he heard the sound of a trumpet being blown very loudly. Fred opened one eye, then, very quickly, he opened his other eye – and then he rubbed both eyes to make sure he was not dreaming.

A little way down the slope of the hill there rode a knight in armour. He was blowing on the trumpet with all his might. His armour was black and his horse was black and he was followed by a little dog, who looked very sad.

The knight stopped blowing and for a moment there was silence.

"Good morning, Sir Knight," said Fred Dragon politely.

"A good morning, is it?" bellowed the knight. "A good morning for fighting dragons!"

He waved his long lance at Fred, who remembered that his father had told him that lots of knights went about the land looking for dragons to fight.

Fred Dragon did not want to fight anybody, but at that

moment the knight pricked the horse with his spurs and they dashed up the hill towards Fred.

Before the knight knew what was happening, the dragon put out a great, red claw and knocked the long lance out of his hand.

"Hey there!" said Fred. "If you must fight me you might at least give me time to get ready."

But the knight was too angry to listen. He turned his horse down the hill a bit, then he drew his heavy sword.

Fred Dragon found that he was very thirsty and he had a quick drink from his stream. He rose to his feet, so that he stood far taller than the knight on horseback, and waited for this strange person to charge again.

"Now," thought Fred. "Perhaps I can think some very angry thoughts about this pesky knight."

He thought very hard, but he did not seem to be getting any hotter. He drew a deep breath and blew as hard as he could. The knight and his horse disappeared in a thick cloud of damp fog.

Fred stared in dismay at the fog. As it slowly cleared away, he saw that the horse, unable to see where it was going in the fog, had collided with a rock and the knight had fallen off. He was sitting on the ground with his helmet all askew, and he looked so funny that Fred laughed and laughed till tears ran down his long nose and splashed on the ground.

"How dare you laugh at me!" shouted the knight, and he grabbed his sword to fight Fred. But the sword had been broken when the knight fell and now, when he shook it at Fred, it was not a heavy sword any more but only a handle. This made Fred laugh even more.

"I don't want to fight you, Sir Knight" he said, when he had managed to stop laughing. "Do let us be friends."

The knight was quite clever, and he now thought up a cunning plan to trick Fred Dragon.

He said, "All right, Dragon. To show you that I am your friend, I will share my sandwiches with you."

"Thank you, Sir Knight," said Fred and he watched while the knight took out a packet of sandwiches and also a pot of pepper. Fred had never seen a pepper pot, so he did not know that the wicked knight was planning to shake the pepper out and when Fred was sneezing, to kill him with his lance.

"Let me put some pepper on your sandwich," said the knight, and Fred was just going to say 'thank you' when the little dog rushed forward and knocked the pepper pot out of the knight's hand.

"Watch out, Mr Dragon," cried the little dog, but he was too late. A cloud of pepper rose up and got into Fred's open mouth. Fred felt his tongue get hotter and hotter. He gave a great roar and – wonder of wonders – a huge sheet of flame shot out of his mouth.

At the sight of the fire-breathing dragon, the nasty knight scrambled onto his horse and galloped away as fast as ever he could.

After a few minutes Fred felt his tongue grow cooler and the flames stopped.

"I did it!" he cried. "I did it!"

The little dog had hidden behind a rock, but now he came out and looked up at Fred.

"What did you do?" he asked.

"I breathed a fire. I breathed a fire!" sang Fred, and he danced about until the whole hill shook and the people in the village ran to their houses in fright.

"You helped me, Little Dog," said Fred. "Thank you for showing me this magic powder."

"That is not magic," said the little dog, "that's pepper."

But Fred knew that it was really magic powder, for after that, whenever he wanted a flame he shook a very little pepper onto his tongue. When it felt good and hot, he blew on the sticks that Little Dog had collected and when they were burning Little Dog made a nice cup of tea. Then Fred Dragon would sit in his nice, warm cave drinking his tea and enjoying himself very much, because now he and Little Dog were good friends and Fred knew that, with a good friend beside him, he would never be lonely again.

FRED DRAGON
AT THE SEASIDE

Fred Dragon was sitting outside his cave and enjoying the warm sunshine when his friend, Little Dog, came slowly up the hill.

"This must be the hottest day of the summer," puffed Little Dog. "You will have to be careful not to blow any big flames, Fred, or you might set the whole hill on fire."

Fred promised not to blow any flames at all and, for a little while, the two friends sat together feeling very warm indeed.

Suddenly Little Dog had a great idea.

"Why don't we go to the seaside?" he cried.

Fred got very excited, because he had never been to see the sea before and he thought it would be a fine adventure.

"I don't know how far away it is" said Little Dog. "But I am sure we could see it if we look from the very top of the hill."

But Fred had a better idea. "Climb up, Little Dog," he said, and when his friend was safely on board, he flapped his great, green wings and rose up into the air. "There it is!" he called, and sure enough, away in the distance, they could see the blue, sparkling sea.

Fred flew quite fast in his excitement and Little Dog held on tightly. Soon they came to the edge of the land and Fred cruised along until he saw a cove where the cliffs curved round each side of a lovely sandy beach. He landed on the sand and found that the cliffs made the cove very private and there was nobody there but themselves.

Fred thought the seaside was wonderful. He paddled in the waves and dug a huge hole in the sand while Little Dog swam in the rock pools and chased seagulls along the shore.

Fred found that all his digging had made him very thirsty, so he took a long drink from a nearby waterfall and then he and Little Dog fell asleep on the soft, warm sand.

Fred was really very tired and he began to snore in his sleep. At each snore he opened his mouth and so, at each snore, he blew out a cloud of damp fog.

On the other side of the cliff there was a small village and the people were amazed to see a patch of cloud drifting out over the blue sea. When they heard Fred Dragon's snores they thought it was thunder, and they were very worried in case the village fishing boats might get caught in a storm. As the snores grew louder and louder, the villagers hid in their houses – all except one little boy. He was called Sandy, and he lived in the village and ran errands for people to earn some money because he had no mother or father to look after him.

Sandy had seen that the puffs of cloud were coming from the cove and he decided to climb up the cliff to try to see what was happening. Imagine his surprise when he looked down into the cove and saw a huge dragon lying asleep with his mouth wide open and breathing great clouds of fog. Sandy was so surprised that he leaned too far out over the edge of the cliff and down he went, giving a loud yell of fright and sending a shower of rocks falling right to the beach. He landed on a little ledge and there he stayed, holding on very tightly to a tuft of grass.

The noise of the falling rocks woke Little Dog, and he looked upwards to see poor Sandy stuck on the narrow ledge.

"Don't be afraid," cried Little Dog. "Fred Dragon will help you down."

Sandy was more surprised than ever when the dog barked in the dragon's ear to wake him up.

"Ha – hrrrrrrrrrrrrrrumph!" snorted Fred, breathing a bigger fog than ever.

"Wake up, Fred," barked Little Dog. "There is a boy stuck up there on the cliff."

Fred Dragon sat up and rubbed his eyes. He saw the fog drifting out to sea and then he looked up and saw Sandy.

"Are you all right, boy?" he asked.

"Yes, sir – Mr Dragon" said Sandy, holding very tightly to the cliff.

"He says he is all right," said Fred sleepily to Little Dog, who jumped up and down with impatience. "And how do you think he is going to get down from there?" he asked.

Then Fred realised what he must do, and he called to Sandy.

"If I reach up and put my head close to you will you climb on to me and hold on tight? I promise I will not let you fall," he added, as Sandy did not look very sure.

"All right, Mr Dragon," said Sandy, because he knew he could not get down from the cliff without help.

Then Fred stretched up his long neck until his head reached the ledge and Sandy scrambled onto the dragon's long nose and up to the top of his head. He held tightly to one of Fred's big ears and was lowered to the ground.

"Thank you very much, Mr Dragon" he said, as he slid off Fred's head to the sand.

"My name is Fred and this is Little Dog" said Fred.

Then Sandy told them about the village people and how they thought there was a storm and were hiding in their houses.

Fred was upset to think that he had frightened anybody and he looked out to sea at the cloud of fog. There was no wind now, so the cloud hung over the water a little way out from the village. "The boats will be stuck out there because there is no wind," said Sandy.

Then Fred had an idea.

"Are you sure all the people are hiding?" he asked, and Sandy said he was sure. Fred took out his pepperpot and peppered his tongue. When it was good and hot, he drew a deep breath and blew. Instead of fog there was a sheet of flame.

"Ooooooooooooh!" cried Sandy.

Fred told Sandy and Little Dog to climb up on his back. Then he flew out to sea and blew gently on the fog, so that in a few minutes it had quite disappeared. By the time he had flown far enough to find the fishing boats, his tongue had cooled down and the flames had stopped.

The fishermen were very frightened when they saw the huge dragon, but Fred flew low over the water and Sandy called to the men not to be scared.

"Hoist up your sails!" he cried. "We will help you to the shore."

When the fishermen saw Sandy, they knew that Fred must be a friendly dragon and they quickly hoisted up their sails. Fred got behind the boats and flapped his great wings up and down. This made a wind, which was so strong that in a minute the boats were sailing merrily towards the harbour.

The village folk ran down to the edge of the sea to watch, and everybody thanked Fred Dragon for bringing the boats safely home. They gave him a basket of fine, fresh fish for his tea.

When Fred and Little Dog were ready to leave, Fred said to Sandy, "Do you not have a home here, Sandy?"

The boy said that though the people were kind to him, he did not have a proper home to call his own.

"How would you like to stay with Little Dog and me for a while?" asked Fred. In a moment Sandy had scrambled onto the dragon's back with Little Dog beside him, and back Fred flew to his cosy cave on the hillside.

That evening Sandy and Little Dog gathered sticks and Fred peppered his tongue just a very little and blew a careful flame to light the fire. They cooked the fish for their tea and later they went to bed in the warm cave and they were all very happy.

Fred and Little Dog were happy because they had a new friend, and Sandy was specially happy because now he had a proper home to call his very own.

FRED DRAGON'S CHRISTMAS

Fred Dragon was very busy. He was getting ready to spend Christmas with his friend Will Woodcutter, who lived in a cottage in the middle of the Great Forest. It was Christmas Eve and Fred, Little Dog and Sandy were all very excited.

They packed the Christmas presents and Little Dog's brush and Sandy's toothbrush and warm pyjamas in a big bag. Then Sandy and Little Dog climbed up onto Fred's scaly back and with the bag between them, they held on tight as the dragon flapped his huge, green wings and rose up into the air.

As Fred flew northwards the weather grew colder, and when they were flying over the Great Forest, they saw that the trees were all laden down with snow. When Fred landed in the clearing where Will's cottage was built, his red feet sank into the soft snow and he shivered so violently that Sandy and Little Dog slid down his side into a snowdrift. They laughed with the fun of it, because Sandy had his big boots and Little Dog had his thick furry coat, but poor Fred was very cold.

Then Will Woodcutter came stumping out of the cottage calling out, "Hello there everybody! I'm very glad to see you."

Sandy and Little Dog wished Will a Merry Christmas. Then they ran to the cottage to see Mrs Will, who gave them hot mince pies to warm their insides.

"Take this special pie out to Fred," she told them.

The pie was so big that Sandy could hardly carry it, but Fred ate it in just one gulp and felt much warmer. He looked at Will Woodcutter and saw that he had a worried frown on his usually cheery face.

"Is something the matter, Will?" he asked.

"Yes indeed Fred," answered Will gloomily. "The snow is so deep that I cannot get to the town to fetch my Christmas shopping."

"Never mind," laughed Fred. "Climb on my back and I'll fly you to town with no bother at all."

"Thanks very much Fred," cried Will, and he hurried back to the cottage where Mrs Will gave him the shopping list and Sandy said he would go along to help.

Little Dog stayed with Mrs Will, and just as the daylight was beginning to fade, there was a sound of flapping wings and he looked out to see that Fred and Will and Sandy had returned. Fred was loaded with sacks and bundles, so that he looked like a new sort of Father Christmas.

Will and Sandy unloaded everything and took it all into the cottage. Then they all had a fine, hot supper and Little Dog and Sandy went to bed.

Will Woodcutter had dug a deep hole in the snow by the side of the cottage and had built up the sides to make a place for Fred, who was much too big to get into the house. Fred lay down on a thick carpet of fir branches that Will had put at the bottom of the hole. He was just thinking how comfy he was when he heard someone whispering.

"Fred Dragon!" hissed Will. "Are you asleep? Something terrible has happened."

"Whatever is it?" asked Fred, scrambling up and shaking off the fir branches.

"We forgot the decorations for the Christmas tree," whispered Will. "I remembered the special candles, but I forgot the shining decorations."

Will was in despair, for he knew that Sandy and Little Dog would be so disappointed. He looked about him as though he would find the answer to his problem somewhere. Then suddenly he saw something lying among the green fir branches that had been Fred's bed.

He picked it up and turned it over. It was like a flat piece of shining silver. It was one of Fred Dragon's scales.

Fred stared at the silver scale, and suddenly he had one of his very best ideas.

"Fetch a big sweeping brush, Will!" he cried, "and bring a basket as well."

Will ran to the cottage and soon returned carrying a brush with stiff bristles. He was followed by Mrs Will, who brought her shopping basket. They had guessed what Fred's good idea was. They climbed up onto his back and Will brushed hard with the broom. Quite a lot of the scales were loose, and before long the basket was full.

Will took a hammer and punched a hole through each scale.

Then Mrs Will put a piece of gold Christmas string through it and hung the scale on the tree.

Will had left a fine tree standing on its own near the cottage and soon it was covered with silver scales that tinkled together as the tree swayed its branches. Then they very carefully put the candles on the tree as well.

They all had a fine time on Christmas day and when the light began to fade, Fred Dragon took the fine new wooden pepper pot that Will had given him and they filled it with pepper that Sandy had given him. When Fred had peppered his tongue and it was good and hot, he blew on the great heap of wood that Will Woodcutter had made and in a very short time there was a wonderful bonfire.

Then Will very carefully lit the candles and they reflected the silver scales, so that the tree seemed to be a magic Christmas tree, shining with a hundred silver flames.

Fred and Sandy and Little Dog with Will and Mrs Will all sat round the bonfire and ate nuts and chocolate and sang Christmas carols, while the stars shone above and the snow shone below and the magic tree shone best of all.

That night Fred Dragon lay on his bed of warm fir branches beside the glowing fire, wrapping himself round with the long, long muffler that Mrs Will had knitted for him.

He went to sleep feeling all warm and comfortable, and was very glad that he had come to spend Christmas in the Great Forest.